Lasting Impressions
What To Tell Your Children

Copyright © 1999 Great Quotations, Inc.

All Rights reserved. Written permission must be secured from the publisher to use or reproduce any part of this book, except for brief quotations in critical reviews or articles.

Compiled By Cheryl Henderson
Cover Illustration by Design Dynamics
Typography by MarketForce, Burr Ridge, IL

Published by Great Quotations Publishing Co.,
Glendale Heights, IL

Library of Congress Catalog Number: 98-75438

ISBN: 1-56245-359-9

Printed in Hong Kong

Dedicated to parents and children everywhere. Choose your thoughts with care and let your words be kind.

Especially for:

_____

Keep your face

to the sunshine

and you will

never see

the shadows.

If you get up one time
more than you fall, you
will make it through.

The first step is
always the hardest.

No one fails who
does his best.

The person who knows everything has a lot to learn.

It is a funny thing about life; if you refuse to accept anything but the best, you very often get it.

Judge each day

not by the harvest,

but by the seeds

you plant.

You have three names:

The name you inherit,
the name your
parents gave you and
the name you
make for yourself.

Create a life you
love to look at.

Knowledge is power.

What can't be done
by advice can often
be done by example.

Some succeed because they are destined to but most because they are determined to.

Your work is a portrait of yourself.

Joyful thoughts create a
joyful world.

Allow your love
to flow freely...
your supply is endless.

The secret of happiness is not
in doing what one likes, but in
liking what one does.

The secret of patience:
Do something else
in the meantime.

Real love always creates,
it never destroys.

The greatest thing
in life is to be needed.

Obstacles are what you see when you take your eyes off of your goal

Be willing to see where change is needed.

The more you love yourself
the more you will
love others.

One person with courage
makes a majority.

Kindness is the overflowing of one's self into the lives of others.

Actions, not words,
are the proof of love.

Courtesy costs nothing
yet it buys things
that are priceless.

Always look for
the good in people.

LEARN TO LISTEN!

Opportunity could be knocking at your door very softly.

Once you have learned to love,
you will have learned to live.

Choose your thoughts
with care.

Every experience in
your life is an
opportunity for growth.

Keep your head
and your heart going in
the right direction and you
will not have to worry
about your feet.

Happiness is the atmosphere in which all good affections GROW.

LIFE
can only be understood
backwards, but it must be
lived forwards.

As soon as you trust yourself,
you will know how to live.

Make the mistakes of yesterday
your lessons for today.

Take time to live because
the world has so much to give.

If you use your time to improve yourself, you will not have time to criticize others.

Take time to laugh, it is the music of the soul.

Some pursue happiness -
others create it.

The most important person
to be honest with
is yourself.

The best
sense of humor
belongs to the
person who can
laugh at himself.

Be "for" things...
not "against" things.

Do what is right
rather than
what is popular.

A misty morning does
not signify a cloudy day.

For every minute
you are angry,
you lose sixty seconds
of happiness.

Be yourself!

Choice, not chance
determines destiny.

Believe in your dreams!

The best way to say
something is to say it,
unless remaining silent
will say it better.

Your mistakes are
your stepping stones
for success.

By the work, one
knows the workman.

The thing to try when all
else fails is try again.

The art of being wise is
the art of knowing what
to overlook.

If the going is getting easier,
you are not climbing.

The right attitude toward
work multiplies achievement.

True wisdom lies in
gathering precious moments
out of each day.

You are not responsible for all things that happen to you, but you are responsible for the way you act when they do happen.

Your preparation of today determines your achievement of tomorrow.

One does not find
happiness in marriage,
but takes happiness
into marriage.

To want what you have
is better than to
have what you want.

Friendship is usually
a plant of slow growth.

Don't ever get so rich
that you can afford
to lose a friend.

When one door closes
another will open.

Don't lose the peace of
years by seeking the
rapture of moments.

As long as you live,
keep learning to live.

Judge everyone with the scale
weighed in his favor.

The weak can never forgive.
Forgiveness is the
attribute of the strong.

Never look down on
anyone unless you're
helping him up.

Never lose a chance of
saying a kind word.

If you do not hope,
you will not find what is
beyond your hopes.

When you think all is lost,
the future remains.

Do not bind yourself to
what you cannot do.

Treat your friends
like family and your family
like friends.

Dig a well
before you are thirsty.

To be happy, do not
add your possessions
but subtract from
your desires.

Do your best and
wait the results in peace.

Hold a true friend with both hands.

You are as successful as you make up your mind to be.

Always

SPEAK THE TRUTH

and you'll never be concerned

with your memory.

Every problem
is an opportunity.

Find yourself, know yourself,
be yourself.

Well begun is half done.

CHARACTER
is like the foundation
to a house, it is
below the surface.

As you think, so you are.

Purpose gives
meaning to life.

If you think you can
or you can't
you're probably right.

REJOICE
in others' successes,
knowing there is plenty
for us all.

Nothing is impossible
to a willing heart.

Temper gets people
into trouble, but pride
keeps them there.

Failure is success
if we learn from it.

You have achieved success
when you have lived long,
laughed often, and loved much.

Cross all bridges with confidence.

Let all your words be kind,
and you will
always hear echoes.

You can give without loving, but you can't love without giving.

If you can find a path with no obstacles, it probably doesn't lead anywhere.

People are less convinced by what
they hear than what they see.

Experience love
wherever you go.

Be kind to unkind people -
they need it most.

The happiness of your life
depends upon the character
of your thoughts.

When you create peace
in your mind, you find it
in your life.

Your aspirations are
your possibilities.

The courage to speak
must be matched
by the wisdom to listen.

Find peace within yourself
and you will not have to
seek it elsewhere.

Forgiveness sets you free.

What we see depends
on what we look for.

Ideas are the
roots of creation.

Success is a ladder
that cannot be climbed
with your hands in your pockets.

What you give out,
you get back.

If you give out only
goodness, in turn, only
goodness comes back to you.

In great attempts
it is glorious
even to fail.

Accept responsibility
for your experiences.

Well done is better
than well said.

To forgive and forget is
far better than to
resent and remember.

Tomorrow is not promised
to us, so take TODAY and make
the most of it.

If you wait to do a great deal
of good at once, you will never
do anything.

Nobody can make you
feel inferior without
your own consent.

The best way to escape
from a problem is
to solve it.

Know who you are and
then be yourself.

You always have
more than you use.

When in doubt,
tell the truth.

The only limits
are those of vision.

A small house will hold as much happiness as a big one.

Appreciation makes most people feel better than almost anything you can give them.

Don't worry about people knowing you, just make yourself knowledgeable.

No matter how far
you have gone
on the wrong road,
turn back.

You are what you
make of yourself.

Know your needs
from your greeds.

Live simply, love well
and take time to smell the
flowers along the way.

Our words may hide our thoughts,
but our actions
will reveal them.

All things are difficult
before they are easy.

Focus on the positive.

You cannot live on hope
alone, nor can you live
without it.

The smallest good deed

is better than the

GRANDEST

good intention.

Remember your past
mistakes just long enough
to profit by them.

Love is never afraid of
giving too much.

If you fail to plan,
you are planning to fail.

REACH

FOR THE

STARS!